les Carnets de Dessins

Henri Scrépel

BARRON'S, WOODBURY, NEW YORK

Printed in France

The pond
1881

National Gallery, Canada
Ottawa

Van Gogh's Universe

Claude Mettra

Ornamental lake in a garden
1888

van Gogh Foundation
Amsterdam

"Wings for gliding above life."

The dark side of life is one many people, as they age, hide beneath the mask of their cares and of their obsessions; but some perceive it with their earliest gaze, as though destined to penetrate to the core of some secret blackness from which nothing will ever distract them. These are the children of the shade, those who from the start are dimly aware of the bitter presence of a hidden order behind the confusion of daily life or the banality of familiar faces. Let us not seek an explanation in the nostalgia for life in the womb which, since Freud, has become the source of our ills. Who can say whether, within his envelope of blood and water, the human child is not crushed by an anguish of which individual existence is only a distant echo. This must be what was perceived by those alchemists of the Renaissance in their efforts to create a homuncule whose principal privilege would be to escape the pangs of conception. The truth is that these children of the shade, far from being reduced to regret for a life before life, are condemned to interpret the moving figures of our becoming.

Vincent Van Gogh belonged to this untamed and solitary cohort, for whom existence is above all a question and a look. But their gaze is often turned aside, early in life, by the solicitous agitation of adults, by the terrifying clutter of word and gesture surrounding their early years. By the time they get to manhood nothing remains but a shadow of melancholy which sometimes falls across the bewilderment of a smile or the brightness of a blue eye which turns fleeting away form the daily round. No such thing threatens Vincent on his emergence into the light of our heavy earth, on the 30 th day of March, 1853. The dwelling was in tune with this silent destiny, as were those who offered him warmth and affection. The presbytery at Groot-Zundert is a house of silence, not the sickly and stifling silence in which so many children cultivate the faded flowers of uncertain desire, but an active silence, in which the still life of the walls and of objects is at one with the murmur of daily life. In this country of wind and water, the houses are a good deal more than mere stops for sleep and family rites, much more than a refuge from the rigours of cold and damp. They represent man's defiance before the hard indifference of the sky, they bear the stamp of that determination to go on existing and to survive despite the unforeseen misfortunes and the mean defeats which every dawn seems to announce.

Farmhouses at Saintes Maries
1888

Museum of Modern Art
New York

In Dutch houses, which are a bit like ships moored upon dry land, the windows play a major role as openings on a restricting horizon from which men strive to remove some part of its ambiguous whiteness. It is through these windows that the men of the country, by nature enterprising, observe the activity of the world, escape from the confines of the home, and listen attentively to many echoes of commerce and exchange. If the domestic interior is invested with a silence so deep that every object becomes the reflection of a human gesture, it is because that peace is a store from which is drawn the strength to face the tasks of the outside world.

But the windows, for the impatience of childhood, are a privileged place of watching and waiting. And indeed the presbytery is a house which does not altogether resemble the others: customs and relationships are not so rigorously limited by social conformity. We do not know the nature of the inner need which led Vincent's father, Theodore Van Gogh, to choose the ministry of God in one of the most deprived parts of the Low Countries. But it may be that, in the heart of this peaceful man, with a taste neither for money nor for travel, and who felt no great need for spiritual enthusiasms, there lived a deep pity for man and the human condition. Here, peasants and working folk walk side by side in poverty, a silent, immemorial poverty which shows in the lines of their faces, in their walk, and in their gaze: and it bears witness to that eternal dialogue between our race and the horrors of the daily round.

Such poverty leaves its traces from one generation to the next, taking no account of emancipation or even prosperity; it is an experience that Vincent Van Gogh knew, as a fascinated spectator, right to the end of his earthly adventure. Poverty of this kind cannot be defined simply in terms of material deprivation or physical decay. It is above all a condition of the whole being, a fundamental humility before the mystery of passion and death, a seemingly dumb acceptance − but one charged with protest and revolt − of the tight-knit web of adversity. Christian meditation alone could give meaning to that poverty within the presbytery at Groot-Zundert. For it is through the vision of Christ, as represented by artists, from the Avignon Pietà to Rembrandt or Georges de la Tour, that poverty is stripped bare, no longer anything but the burning image of real life, a life which is hidden, freed from all its disguises and all its masks. In this sense, Van Gogh's long quest might seem a pitiful attempt to track down poverty and force it to reveal its strange secret. It is the link that binds together the first representation of peasant life and the self-portraits of his final years: behind the faces of the ploughmen and the haymakers, behind the pursuit of his own image, what Van Gogh seeks is the naked Christ, bearing witness to that passionate anguish which is the end-product of all inner knowledge.

The whole of Van Gogh's life shows a deepening of this first revelation; his painting will come late and fleetingly, a few years bounded by a lingering adolescence and a death which is like a song of victory in the brilliance of the final summer; it endows the revelation with its final meaning, submits it to the critical gaze of other men, but also exorcises the evil forces which might lead him away from his central concern. And his life is uneventful in the sense that it seems implicitly to obey some need which leaves no room for elements which might divert him from the path which leads from the shades of childhood to the final illumination. Uneventful indeed, but not free of these trials or expectations, or searching calamities, which never fail to strike those who refuse to be on their guard, or who, like Van Gogh round about his twenty-fifth year, accept to expose themselves to those misfortunes which circle with unending vigilance around our lives.

Vincent Van Gogh is not unaware of the uncertainties and the contradictions through which we must pick our way towards our true self. Our childhood universe may well be an enclosed terrain where we see our being reflected in our own untamed nature, it may be that the human offspring can feed on its own violence without experiencing terror before the violence of the world; but with adolescence begins the hazardous journey through the temptations, the passions, and the incoherences of the adult world. In the midst of those conflicting influences, the young man must discover how to assert his individuality, and how to exploit that sun whose warmth he feels within him. Much later in life, Vincent Van Gogh will remember these unsettled years lived in the diminished shadow of a family suddenly deprived of the charm it has when one is young: "Sometimes a man has a glowing hearth at the centre of his soul and no one ever comes to warm himself at it and passers-by notice only a little smoke drifting upwards, from the chimney, and then continue on their way... And what should one do but keep up the fire inside, have salt within oneself, wait patiently, though with great impatience, await the moment when whoever feels like it will come to sit there, and will remain. May whoever believes in God await the hour which sooner or later will come." The language of desire, the tumult of a glance which attempts, in the inextricable weave of tangled existences, to make out the sign intended for it alone.

The desire which never finds its object, the constantly broken thread by which men discover in adulthood that which will never belong to their world, such is the apprenticeship of life. The stages on Van Gogh's way, once he has left school, were in the Goupil galleries in The Hague, London, Paris, and London once again, before he returned to his birth-place at Christmas 1876. These years of exile, snatching him away from the old familiar landscapes of his native province, drove Van Gogh in upon himself and compelled him to live a prisoner of that timidity from which travel and work should

On the Rhône
1888

Staatliche Graphische Sammlung
Munich

The beach at Saintes Maries
1888

van Gogh Foundation
Amsterdam

have freed him once and for all. The spectacle of great cities, far from attuning him to the fortunes and the pleasures or urban life, served only to surround him with the many faces of misery. Three companions accompany him in his hazardous journey through these Western capitals: the crowd, woman, and God. And all three meet his restlessness with the same silence. In London and in Paris, he contemplates the mass of men, and seeks within them the painful familiarity which, throughout his childhood, drew him close to his fellow-countrymen. But those Dutch peasants were for him a living genealogy: a genealogy of blood, it is true, but also of gesture, speech, and silence − and it is this that he will try to convey in his first Dutch sketches. The pallid beings he meets as he walks through the highly coloured parts of the town are nothing more for him than naked misery, exile without name. What words could reach the spark, the secret fire hidden within them?

Only one universe is open to the man dazzled by the deep glow dormant in the hearts of strangers, and that is the world of prostitutes. Not that Vincent Van Gogh had not tried to live that complicity of the heart, that sovereign intimacy which, through the privileges granted to one other being, makes it possible to break free from one's own inner divisions, and to transfer to that person the responsibility of bearing the intolerable burden of one's life. In London, he fails with Ursula, just as, later on in Holland, he will meet disaster with Kate or Sein. Beyond the refusal suffered at the hands of women lies the land of prostitution. Van Gogh no doubt did no more than skirt round this land for a long time. The attraction for him was not the flesh, nor was it the Baudelairean obsession with degradation. It was much more the certainty that the world of prostitution, symbolising all the upheavals of life, is a negative of conventional existence, on which the imagination can work without hindrance, and through which it is possible constantly to reinvent creation. As Julien Green has written: "Purity can be found only in Paradise or in Hell." In the infernal theatre to which his long walks through dark alleys draw him every night, in the contemplation of destinies which, through the bodies of the damned, create new dream-patterns, Van Gogh's eyes fixed upon what he had sought behind the stained glass of Dutch houses: the traces of an elementary and archaic humanity, reduced to a simple sign.

It is true that this cold world of loose women in no way penetrates the life of Van Gogh during his periods in London and Paris. It remains a background whose true nature he will invent rather than discover. Indeed, it represents that ultimate solitude of the heart from which Van Gogh attempts to defend himself in his disastrous adventure with Ursula − the first in a series of similar desertions suffered by him in the following years.

"Evil, a terrible evil in this world and in ourselves."

The summer of 1874, in London, is given over entirely to the wreck of his passion for Ursula. The dark arches of churches were the only witnesses of his distress. In November of the same year, he is back in The Hague, restored to the spiritual climate of his childhood. That winter is a gap, an interlude for reflection, from which he will emerge in the Spring of 1875 in order to go to Paris, where he will have some contact with the Impressionists and rediscover his favourite painters in their native setting: the painters of popular life, such as the Le Nain brothers and Chardin; but above all the artist who will always be for him the great master of the life of the people, Millet: his themes will always be present in the work of Van Gogh, who will continue his patient quest along the most unexpected paths. But his stay in Paris is short. Even more than in London, the artificial world of dealers and collectors must have seemed to Van Gogh an abyss, breaking and disfiguring those who fall into it. The following Spring, he is back in England; his life as an art dealer is completely at an end. Plunged into a working-class area of Ramsgate he works as teacher and as a preacher − a shepherd for the innocent, the outcast, and the slave. The task is thankless, and faces him each day with the implacable condition of men: physical misery, wretchedness of the heart, distortion of hopes and of dreams. Like a messiah who does not yet know what truths he should communicate, he seeks the words with which to restore the true light to a poverty-stricken people; but he remains as though dumb in a forest of deaf men. His words call forth an echo in himself alone, and that echo is of the cruellest kind.

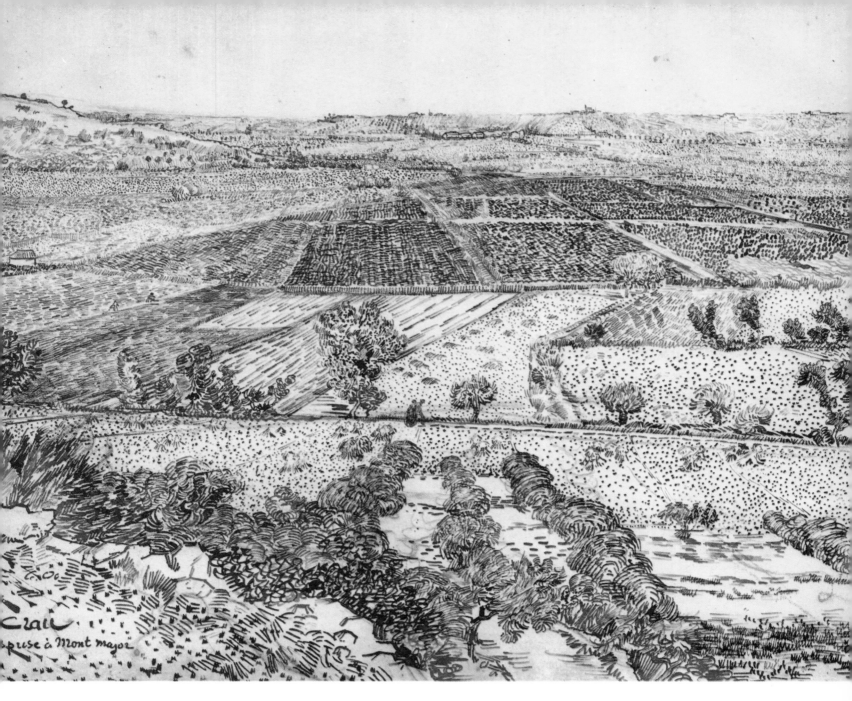

The Crau, as seen from Montmajour
1888

van Gogh Foundation
Amsterdam

As the years go by between his sixteenth year when, as an adolescent, he want to live in The Hague, and his twenty-fourth, when he returns to his native land, so the gulf grows wider between Van Gogh and that life which helps others to make sense of the difficult pattern of needs, desires, and hopes.

In July 1876, in one of his last letters from England, he writes: "I am going astray in a number of ways, but I must not despair." A year later, he says in a letter to his brother, Theo: "When I think of the past, when I think of the future, and of the difficulties which all seem to me insoluble... then I too am tempted to give up." Give up what, and to do what?

At the end of 1876, he is back in Holland for Christmas. After the zeal which, up till then, had kept him going in the Ramsgate mists, he falls victim to an immense fatigue. He returns home in a state of physical and nervous breakdown. But whether impassioned or in a state of collapse, this man whose gaze is still the home of child-like tenderness gives more and more the impression of drifting slowly towards the dark world of madness. He is easily convinced that he should not go back to England but take a job as salesman in a Dordrecht bookshop. This winter is a long season of waiting: Vincent is very much alone, he plunges into reading the Bible, makes numerous visits to churches, and sometimes at night, when sleep will not come, he draws. His hope is that, amongst those men who have given themselves to the service of God, he will find that brotherly bond which brings peace and reassurance to the senses and the heart. In order to reach them, he will not hesitate to pay the price that is asked. In May, he is in Amsterdam to follow a course at the Faculty of Theology. For a whole year, he remains immersed in the unplumbed boredom of textbooks, and in the dust of exegesis. It is a hollow world, in which living words end up desiccated and dead, just as the hope of the evangelists also seems dead. In the depths of man there is something more than a vague belief in redemption. In the depth of Van Gogh, there is a burning brightness, a wound, but where, oh where is life?

Work in the vineyards
1888

van Gogh Foundation
Amsterdam

"Here it is the sick who care for the sick, and the pauper who is the friend of the poor."

In the Autumn of 1878, in an attempt to flee this emptiness, this trough, this suddenly ended pause, he takes refuge in the Borinage, and lives as a pauper amongst the poor, as a naked heart in the midst of other hearts for ever laid bare. The people he finds there seem to him the same as those he knew, many years before, in the bewildered peace of the presbytery of Groot-Zundert. The road to the Borinage marks the end of a long mystical turmoil, which had its hidden beginning in London after the disastrous passion for Ursula, continued in Paris, through his ceaseless meditation on sacred texts, and his reading of works inspired by the great Romantics − particularly Michelet − and which now emerged into full light during his stay amongst the miners.

What he went through was a gradual turmoil rather than a crisis, for it was indeed a reversal of his whole being, a wrench away from the provisional reassurance that makes it possible for men to follow the road forward without constantly falling into that absence of the self which is the antichamber to suicide. Van Gogh's history before and after his adventure in the Borinage is a history of dislocation. The external world − that of other people, who are both his brothers and his enemies − becomes infected with a painful alienation. That reality which we apprehend through our experience of daily life begins to dissolve: who are these beings who go about their work, or their sorrows, or their pleasures, but whose words now come from a great distance and are no more than the muffled echo of a lost order? Van Gogh is doubly isolated: separated both from the world and from himself, for he is lucid enough to perceive himself in the light of that estangement which falls on other men. He has the feeling that a barrier has insidiously and patiently risen between his own life and that of society. But where does that place him? On which side of the barrier? Has not a whole part of himself been driven towards that ill-defined and imprecise horizon, to which men drift, like shades, unable to discover the sign which might lead them back to a comprehensible world?

The Hospital Garden
1888

van Gogh Foundation
Amsterdam

Houses at Saintes Maries
1888

van Gogh Foundation
Amsterdam

This loss of identity, this certainty of a dissolution of the self against which there is no defence, lead him to the point where, faced with his own existence, he is thrown into a state of fear and of panic. His mind is adrift, and before long, his body, too, experiences the dizziness of the castaway. To what can he cling but the most humble figures of every day life, the silent companions of sleepless nights and crowded days, of impatient dawns and calm dusks – in other words objects, things. The obsession with what the French stupidly refer to as *nature morte*, but which the English and the Germans call "still life", here has its full significance: objects are the mediators which make it possible for man to restore the dialogue with himself, and to succeed, at least in part, in finding a new place for himself in the general movement of life. For Van Gogh, it provides the means by which he may confront the impenetrable world of things, and rediscover the slow presence of that reality which the fantasies of the mind can never reach. But it is only later, through the practice of his art, that he will know the warmth of objects, burning in its intensity to those who know how to penetrate to their naked intimacy. During his experience of the Borinage, his concerns are of another kind. In the great confusion of all his senses, in the fragmentation of his physical and mental nature, this man who is not yet an artist, and who is faced with a reality which eludes him, another reality, must attempt both to destroy and to reconstruct himself.

The means with which he can make the attempt are slim. They are based almost entirely upon a return to the time when the world could be understood, to those seasons in which mankind inhabited a coherent landscape and in which words and gestures had their full significance. The Borinage was an effort to restore childhood, but childhood made simple and pure, so that strangers from the big city, the over-rich countryside, the mysterious sea, could all be swept into the shade. All who remain are companions from a dream which feeds on distant imaginings, they are the men and the women of the black earth, who direct our gaze to their feet rather than to their face – for they walk bent double, not through servility of heart or body, but because the earth, which is both their cradle and their grave, is at the same time their sole source of warmth and companionship. The shoes they wear are not the pathetic though necessary protection of people who wander the streets or journey across the frozen countryside, they *are* the men who wear them. That is why, when Van Gogh draws shoes, he gives them almost human form. For him they are not mere objects lost amongst the tools of daily life. They may be revealed in their solitude without thereby becoming absurd. Their appeal, emerging from their gaping, intimate blackness, invites the wanderer to depart – but to what nocturnal roving?

It will lead to the miners and the peasants of the Borinage, men of his own sort, who will make of Van Gogh an artist and a painter. He needed this trial to purge him of all the temptations which had assailed him in urban life, above all, perhaps, the temptation to become an artist like those he had known, and no doubt loved, during his years of apprenticeship as an art dealer. The trial emerged above all as a need for extreme self-denial. The pastoral vocation is seemingly a way of

becoming absorbed into the memory of his father, of identifying himself with the banal, insipid face of the former pastor of Groot-Zundert. But the path which must be followed is more complex: masks, desires, memories must all play their part in the attempt to discover whether, after the disaster, there will remain anything of the man.

It is in no way evangelical self-denial (to use an extremely vague expression) that brings Vincent to the Borinage. Leaving London or Paris is not so much a sacrifice as a liberation, for the urban landscape with its intense agitation, just as much as the rhetoric of the art galleries, seems a dark pit in which he can no longer even make out his own face. The reasons for his departure are more closely linked with his determination to depart from himself and to offer himself as a prey to hunger and thirst, in order at the same time to submerge the worn-out image he has of himself, and the image the world is beginning to have of him. Van Gogh's one certainty is that somewhere, hidden in the depths of being, there must exist some spark, some hidden fire; if it is to be restored to the light of day, it can only be through the abolition of the self, through the destruction of the individual, along with the whole arsenal of gestures, words and dreams which are no more than the cumbersome heritage of habit. He goes towards the miners and the ploughmen because he believes them to be the greatest victims of hunger and thirst; but also because, for them, he is nothing if he is not one of them, a destiny without individual meaning, without identity.

In the Borinage, men are like those villages which "look desolate, abandoned, dead, because life is concentrated beneath the earth and not above". In order to be like them, he destroys, he burns himself. The question he seeks to answer through his experience of penury is the one asked some time earlier by Dostoievsky in his writer's Diary: "What is the point of organizing one's life and devoting so much effort to settling into human society in a way which shall be regular, reasonable and completely right? The only answer that can be made is: in order to procure pleasure for myself. But if, as is at present the case, I constantly ask myself such questions, then I cannot be happy"; and beyond this interrogation, the Russian writer discovers the immense mockery of human pity, for "we wilfully bring to mind a strange thought of an intolerable sadness: what if man was put on earth for purely experimental reasons, just to see if such a being can or can not live in this world? What makes this thought so particularly melancholy is once again the fact that no one is responsible, that no one has tried such an experiment, that no one is to blame, but rather that everything has happened simply because of the inanimate laws of nature − laws which for me are totally unintelligible and to which my mind will never succeed in becoming accustomed".

Wooded hill
1888

van Gogh Foundation
Amsterdam

Field behind the Hospital
1889

Staaliche Graphische Sammlung
Munich

If there exists some reality in opposition to the absurdity of nature, its mystery will be unveiled by those who belong to the oldest tribe, those people who labour in obscurity for generations without end. While in the Borinage, Van Gogh becomes a great reader of Michelet, not so much as historian of France, but rather as the author of books about nature, and in particular the essay which he first called *Le Ventre*, but then published under the title *Woman*. Michelet insists upon the long gestation of this earth, and upon the part men play in the act of creation. For creation is not complete, but goes on throughout the ages: in this evolution, men are actors, not merely passive lookers-on. The great adventure of life develops through a genealogy in which each living being has its place. The evangelist of the Borinage does not yet do more than suspect the existence of such a genealogy. Drawing, then painting, will help him to transform the suspicion into certainty, the intuition into an objective. "The objective will become better defined, will slowly and surely take form, just as the outline becomes a sketch, the sketch a picture, the more one works seriously on it, the more one penetrates the surface."

The company of humble people teaches Van Gogh that they need neither pity nor words, but rather a much more silent force capable of taking root in the furthest depths of their experience of the world. That is the only form of love adequate to their ancestral anguish. And indeed of what use is love except to give a countenance to the loved one, to restore him to a hitherto unknown world of truth, to give a place in the sun to all that has existed only in night. And it is in order to bring its share of love to the crushed humanity around him that he begins urgently to draw. The creatures of the shade emerge from the shade, but still only through the black of the pencil. Many years will pass before the shade is embellished with the heart-rending colours which enclose the tragedy of the world.

The difficult beginnings of his creative work bear witness before all else to the fact that Vincent Van Gogh does not accept himself as an artist. He does not yet know what privileges bestow upon the image of misery and anguish a reality greater than that of misery and anguish themselves. Is there not something derisory in the presence of art before the forces of evil? It is as though he allowed himself the unmerited liberty of looking at and representing the destiny of those companions whom no one may deprive of the one right they possess: the right to silence. That is why the whole year in the Borinage is a year of expiation: he gives of himself unstintingly to come to the aid of those around him, and more than neglects the needs of his own body. In fact, he submits himself to a form of physical and mental penitence which is all the more dangerous in view of his already seriously diminished nervous state. But the privation into which he sinks more and more will slowly free him from his evangelical obsessions, and urge him gently towards that universe in which he will find himself alone with a series of unformed images which seek expression, alone with a revelation which must take form.

Scene of Arles
1888

Museum of Art
Rhode Island School of Design
Providence

"A prisoner in I know not what horrible, horrible, very horrible cage."

Gradually, through the twists and turns of his pilgrimage, Van Gogh devotes himself less to pastoral care and more to drawings. He had tried to lose himself in the still, unchanging, incurable misery of others. Now he is thrown back upon his own affliction, condemned to retreat within the frontiers where he cannot be reached by others, and with no means of subsistence other than his own strength, his own hopelessness. A letter written to Theo in the summer of 1880 shows more than clearly that this solitude has crushed him and that he has drifted more and more rapidly away from those shores upon which he could maintain a form of behaviour familiar to other people. What he asks is that others should show him a little of the pity he has for them, that they should not allow him to drift completely out of reach, as in olden days the sick in mind were cast off in the ship of fools. He himself has no very clear picture of the road he was following, he has no great certainties which might calm the concern of those who care for him and love him in their own way. But is he not enclosed behind the impenetrable shutter of his own fate? "In Spring, the caged bird knows full well that something good exists, it is aware that there is something which should be done, but it cannot do it or know exactly what to do. It cannot quite remember, and then has some shadowy ideas and says to itself: "the others build nests, and have chicks, and bring up their brood; and it strikes its head against the bars of the cage. But the cage remains and the bird becomes mad with grief".

The grief is the darkness in the depth of the mind, the confusion of muscles and nerves in the breakdown of the body. A thin partition separates the flame at the centre of the being of the kingdom of unreason. This is perhaps the start of what is usually called Van Gogh's intrusion into the land of madness, but it would be much more correct to speak of the start of his victory over madness. For the ten years which separate Van Gogh from his death, far from being no more than the history of his affliction, should on the contrary be seen as an act of defiance against all the powers of evil, and against all the corrupting ferment of the mind. Far from giving way to those wounds which leave man helpless in the face of his personal disaster, Van Gogh shows, both in his life and in his work, the lucid accomplishment of a fundamental project which consists of a search to the limits of the self in order to discover what exactly is meant by life, and death, and human destiny. Throughout those ten years and up to the so carefully devised death, what we witness is the progress of a sovereign consciousness, always

Rough pen-drawing
on a letter from van Gogh

van Gogh Foundation
Amsterdam

extraordinarily active, and alive to anything which might nourish what people will call his genius, or his revelation, or his illumination − but which, in any case, can in no way be said to owe its existence to what is thought of as madness.

Van Gogh's illness has often been compared to Nietzsche's madness; such a comparison is as mistaken for the philosopher of Sils Maria as for the painter of the Aliscamps. It is true that on a particular day in 1889 Nietzsche's reason turns towards uncertain horizons, where his illness will keep him forever separated from the community of man. But in terms of the history of the work of creation − and whatever name the doctors may give to Nietzsche's adversity, or whatever indication it may give of his final afflictions − his work in the period before the Turin crisis is in no way the work of a madman; on the contrary, it bears witness to his striking awareness and lucidity; far from belonging to the world of darkness, it stands out in the full light of day. Too high a degree of awareness and too great a concentration on the blaze of the sun can certainly lead to loss of one's reason; Nietzsche himself had such a foreboding before he foundered, as he showed when he wrote: "Farewell, I have seen further than is my right." And indeed the reader of his work may observe that his madness is itself nothing more than an accident which

28

Boats at Saintes Maries
Musée d'Art Moderne

Brussels

interrupts the rhythm of his life. Van Gogh's evolution is along the same lines. Like the prophet of Zarathoustra, he will until the end remain unmoving in the full light of the spirit.

It is true that the story of these ten years is not part of what is thought of as normal life. But we now know what a flimsy, insubstantial barrier stands between those destinies which some see as normal, and others as pathological. That is not to deny the existence of those bottomless pits where men are completely given over to disorders of the mind, and where neither word nor gesture can make contact with the absent spirit: such will be the final fate of Nietzsche. There is, however, no parallel in the case of Van Gogh. His experience is that of a painful dual dialogue in which he fears that he may lose his grip, while at the same time succeeding in clinging on at the very edge of the abyss. He lives this difficult dialogue with himself, with physical weariness, the hopelessness of sleepless nights, doubt, isolation of the flesh, and the old obsessions of childhood which return to haunt him in his adult years. There is also the difficulty of the dialogue with other people: the barren round of daily tasks and privations, and all those other painful preoccupations − food, money, drink, tobacco, but also contempt, indifference, incomprehension. Do not such disorders fill the life of many of our fellow-men? We know perfectly well that it is the case, and when we find ourselves face to face with a being momentarily disturbed by the insistent murmuring of life, we quickly turn aside to avoid the sight of our own double.

Thus, the ten years that Van Gogh devotes to painting should not be explained in terms of a gradual penetration of sickness into a life open to countless dangers, but rather by a deepening of his creative consciousness which will lead him from the shade-filled countryside of his Dutch period to the unbearable light of the years spent in Provence. The journey from night to dazzling day was bound to be a journey filled with terrors, for there can be no comfort in the progress through the night of the mind towards one's personal dawn. Nietzsche, too, experienced the dark period of travelling (during which, he said, the sky remains obscured for long stretches before help comes from the feeblest shaft of light) − and before breaking through to that song of victory called "Dawn". But such trials are to be found on the chart of any interior voyage, they are a necessary part of that exploration whose end is always before us, even though it may frequently be obscured. It is a truth which Van Gogh quickly perceived, as he showed in writing: "This is how I see things: I must go on, go on, that is what is necessary." And if Nietzsche and Van Gogh indeed have anything in common, it must surely be the fascination with something that is always in the future, which draws them forward, but at the same time demands enormous sacrifices from them along the way. That is why the creative genius is so often no more than a series of crises, and why so many fruitful lives are overwhelmed by pain. It is the price which must be paid for the unforeseeable discovery announced by Hölderlin: "It must reveal itself, that great secret which will bring me either life or death."

30

Orchards in Provence
1888

van Gogh Foundation
Amsterdam

"The man who has been wounded by an unhappy love will always rise once more to the surface."

In the summer of 1880, Van Gogh has not yet realised that both the meaning and the end of his adventure are to be found in the revelation of the light and in his intrusion into the solar regions. All he knows is that it is fate which has made it possible for him to escape from a total breakdown and once more to find at least some energy and love of life. And as though he wished to justify himself in the eyes of those around him, who have no idea what to think of his strange behaviour, he settles in Brussels and registers himself at the Academie des Beaux-Arts. What he hopes is that, with patient effort, he will succeed in learning to draw according to accepted conventions, and so begin to live by his work, if only modestly. The hope is one he tries to make Theo and his father share with him. He finds it difficult to reconcile what he wants to do and what is asked of him, especially since his natural inclination is towards his own desires rather than to the customs of the Academy. In the Spring of 1881, he notes: "In general, the peasants, and the bourgeoisie suspect of evil and of black designs any man who, in the sole hope of discovering picturesque scenes and remarkable faces, carries out his searches in those places, those corners and those holes which others prefer to avoid. A peasant who watches me drawing a tree-trunk, and who sees me work for an hour without moving, imagines that I am mad and makes fun of me." At any rate, the effort he makes to find a place − even a humble place − in the tasks carried out by other men, helps to make his family forget the sort of terror they had experienced when they saw him plunging into a mystical search which might lead to unforeseen excesses. In April 1881, as much to restore his childhood link with his family as to escape from the material obligations of life in Brussels, he goes to Etten, near Breda, where his parents had been living for six years. That spring was for him a time of work and of profound peace. He draws landscapes and people. He looks forward to improving his state of health, devotes much time to reading, and goes for long walks in the country. It proves to be a short interlude in the cruel succession of seasons: during the summer, this solitary man, who was only just opening his eyes once more to the joys of this world, fell in love with one of his nieces, Kee Vos-Stricker, who had recently lost her husband and was living at the Etten presbytery with her child. Once more, an abyss opens before Van Gogh.

The rock
1888

van Gogh Foundation
Amsterdam

Up to this point, the world of sensuality had been reduced to silence. In that Dutch house, the voice of the flesh was covered by the humble sound of daily prayers, and hidden beneath the peaceful dialogue with work and with objects. As a child, Van Gogh had been violently aware of the depth of those images which smothered any awareness of the body. His youthful years had been lived in the greatest solitude, and in total introspection; in the eternal confrontation with himself, it was the body which had defined the limits of his world. He knew no word to describe desire, but it is easy for us to guess its intensity. Throughout his life, it will make itself heard like a long complaint. That is why there are so few female nudes in the long succession of works produced by him: for Van Gogh, women stand for his oldest secret, for he has the vague hope that one day he may be able to violate their distant intimacy. The few nudes produced by him all belong to his Paris period, a time of distraction and retreat when his artistic themes lose their privileges as they are led astray by the confusion of the city.

It is in the tragedy of his sensuality that we may seek both the sign and the source of Van Gogh's misfortunes. Through his body, the child and then the adolescent make an appeal to those around him: it brings no response, and never will. His early fascination with peasant-women is the fevered expression of a passionate body which does not yet know the secrets of sexuality, but which suspects that, within those simple lives, given over to the sun, to the rain, to the shifting winds and the rhythms of the sky, there must also be found a simple life of the senses. The whole of rural life is an echo of the elemental relationship between men and nature, and a constant reminder of the intermingling of forms of life. Even for a child still blind to grown-up complicity, the symbols of present life are so many evocations of the action of the body; milk, seed, sweat, the odours of man and beast, all of these provoke a young imagination to invent without the experience of physical stimulation. This imagination finds a heightened form in a kind of transformation of the individual from actor into spectator − in other words, *voyeur*. Since he cannot penetrate his own sensuality, he must spy on that of others, and try to make a forced entry into that hidden universe which is the setting for a drama in which the characters are hidden by masks.

At what point of existence begins the separation between the imperative awareness of the flesh and the certainty of a prohibition which condemns that flesh to darkness? In the case of Van Gogh, it comes well before puberty. Georg Groddeck, speaking of schizophrenia (that schizophrenia which, according to Karl Jaspers, explains the painter's illness), defines it as the break between what he calls the soul of the belly and the soul of the heart. For most people, those who are not ill, without necessarily being in good health, the break comes early and without great damage. But in some, who are of a particularly nervous disposition, it can happen very late and cause great pain. Van Gogh is

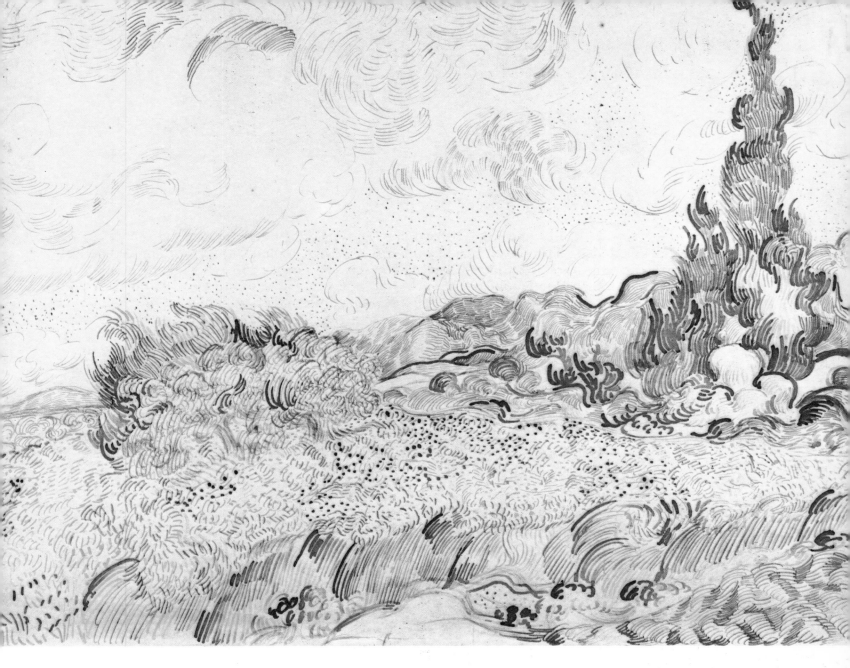

Cornfield and Cypress-Tree
1889

van Gogh Foundation
Amsterdam

Corner of the park
1888

van Gogh Foundation
Amsterdam

such a man: for the child, the soul is situated in the belly because that is where he came from, and because his own belly, more than any other part of his body, is his personal kingdom. By retaining his soul in his belly instead of situating it in his heart, he remains faithful to his distant origins, and defines his relationship with the world in terms of his physical body, rather than in terms of feeling or memory. A being who is this way identified with his belly – that is to say with his flesh – cannot conceive of sensuality as the extension of an inner turmoil or ecstasy. On the contrary, he puts the action of the senses at the start of every dialogue with other people. Van Gogh's devotion to prostitutes arises from this elementary fact: the prostitute represents primitive innocence in that she is flesh and not feeling, the gift of the body and not the demands of the heart. The great though painful priority which the child or the adolescent gives to the belly is a way of expressing his great desire for freedom, that sovereign freedom of which Rimbaud was undoubtedly the prophet. For the heart, like the head, is indeed the terrain where others, those outside oneself, break in with a brutality which may not always be perceived, but which is the cause of so many childhood wounds.

Georg Groddeck sees the voice of the belly as the expression of the naïve part of our nature, and contrasts it with the head and the heart, which are concerned with social convention. But how may we reconcile ourselves to it when the outside world so frequently frustrates it? Van Gogh's answer lies in the intensity of his religious life, in his sense of mystical wonder. While in the Borinage, it is through Christ, as mediator between nature and human flesh, that he justifies his fundamental exile from the world of reality in which society seeks to enclose him. Christ is not a moral prophet. He is the Messiah who announces the reconciliation of the individual body with the body of the cosmos: in his final canvases, through his copies of Rembrandt, Van Gogh will replace the face of Christ with an immense sun. This man, who is not yet a painter, addresses his prayers, not to the calculating and cruel God of the church, but rather to a Christ incarnate, who came temporarily to earth, and who provides the link between the moving substance of the world and the metamorphosis of the living.

We know little of the mystical ardour in which Van Gogh's adolescence took refuge. We may gain a glimpse of it in what, a few years later, becomes the evangelism of the Borinage. At that time, he is already plunged into an enormous amount of reading: and that alone sets him apart both from his family environment and, later on, from the painters and art-lovers who are to be found in the different branches of the Goupil galleries. His feverish desire for knowledge leads him to read all those who have borne witness to man's unending divisions, but who fail to console him for that dislocation which he obscurely experiences within himself as the reason why the body seems to withdraw to such a distance from the temptations of the heart.

But by bestowing such an essential priority upon the body, upon his belly, he is attempting to endow it with the same purity, the same almost abstract rigour, as that of the mind. Whence the very early temptation to reduce the demands of his physical organism to the minimum. There can be no doubt that Van Gogh finds it easy to justify the privations he imposes on his own body by taking refuge behind the mask of piety. But behind his insistence upon privation there lies a desire which bears

little resemblance to religious asceticism. The obstinacy with which he refuses food is not, as for the true ascetic, a means of attaining grace, but rather an end in itself, a test of his own limits. It may be interpreted as a thirst for self-destruction. But it is also evidence of an extraordinary pride, and of a need to reduce his body to a sort of sketch, as a means of transforming it into an exhilarating star. These privations were not intentional when Van Gogh was alone in Nuenen, Antwerp, or Arles, but became deliberate when he was in London; when he reappeared in Etten, his family was appalled by his state of physical decrepitude. Van Gogh discovers a means of keeping his solar body, while at the same time opening it to the promise of earthly life. That means is what he will call love, and it is the explanation of his passion for Kee.

The passion is one he lived with staggering intensity. It was a refuge from the years of exile he had suffered since childhood. It led to reconciliation with the peaceful Dutch countryside, and entry into a Kingdom which had so far remained closed to him. It also brought reconciliation with himself, for ever since childhood he had feared himself and lived in dread of the abyss towards which his disorder drew him. "Never, no, out of the question" is Kee's response, to which he replies "her and no other". Throughout those weeks in the summer of 1883 he maintains a vague hope, in defiance of the total refusal of the one who will always be for him the woman; and, for the first time perhaps, he experiences a strange peace, a calm which colours the future. Is it simply that the fire within him consumes his own suffering? Is it no more than the reverse side of that intolerable anguish that haunts his nights when he realises that nothing can break the circle of his solitude?

"Passions are the sails of the boat, you see"; but in the winter of 81, the passions burn in a void, and the boat drifts away, without sails, towards the blackest night. Nothing could stop Kee from sinking into that blackness. But the solitude is unbearable. Kee, the image of calm beauty, of fertile silence, of the happy interior, gives way to anonymous poverty − the prostitute Sein, crushed by boredom, wretchedness, disease: "a pregnant woman, wandering the streets in the attempt to earn her bread in the way you can guess". Kee is far away, and refuses to see him. The pitiful prostitute was there, plunged in need. For two full years, this untamed man will attempt to restore a life to a being whose existence is no longer anything but a collection of dispersed fragments.

In this calm mingled with the most frightful material difficulties, the artisan rediscovers his identity, the worker returns to his task: "Speak to me about nothing but one thing: drawing. She also has a steady job: posing." Van Gogh's only ambition is to be an expert workman, like those he sees every morning setting off along the quayside in The Hague. Then, little by little, this life, intended as a life like any other, falls victim to erosion. The poor prostitute becomes transformed into that nightmare room whose walls close in as though to stifle life. Nothing remains but to set off once more into the night streets, bearing in his heart the great burden of those things to which he has failed to give life.

Cornfield behind the Hospital
1889

Nationalgalerie
East Berlin

Thistles
1888

van Gogh Foundation
Amsterdam

werbeds in a garden
8

Gogh Foundation
sterdam

Field behind the Hospital
1889

Kröller-Müller Stichting
Otterlo

"Each man must cut the knot for himself."

The double tragedy of Etten and The Hague finally brings to an end what might be called Van Gogh's personal biography − all those events and accidents which combine to form the story of one life within the history of a century. From this time on, he will remain within the circle from which everything that seems to have no direct link with his art will apparently be excluded. The circle will become increasingly smaller and he will no longer be able to avoid destroying himself by crashing into its bounds. His love for Kee had promised entry into the Garden of Eden, his adventure with Sein had been a horrifying pilgrimage through the suburbs of pity. From now on, the world of other people will have no meaning for him; each day brings further destruction of the man; the artist is finally restored to that territory which belongs to him alone. The mental kingdom finds itself freed from all the cares which encumbered it. It is true that, right until the end, the "old man" will remain, caught up in the disasters of life, and an impotent witness to the erosion of time: a body wearing itself out through privation, the unsuccessful attempts to find a time and a place to escape from destruction, the occasional obscure temptation to be a man like other men... This "old man" can do no more than live out a cruel, banal, abandoned life with a body incapable of anything but pain; but there is also a Van Gogh, known to the masters of hermetic wisdom as the "Ancient" ("archivieux"), who transcends the daily disaster in his search for inexpressible knowledge.

There are indeed many bridges leading from the "old man" to the "Ancient". And the theme of the bridge, taken up by Van Gogh in one of his last canvases, is a good illustration of the link between the various stages of his awareness. The bonds between the near and the distant parts of life are all the closer since they seem both to suffer from the same affliction: as Antonin Artaud will point out later on, there is a sort of dust which eats into the visible world as well as into the dark regions of the mind. But beyond evil there is always something which remains protected from corruption and, as Hölderlin wrote, "that which remains is perpetuated by poets". The road is no easy one to travel: it is close to that of the gnostics, who followed it through the darkness in their attempt to produce the brief flash of enlightenment. It is of no great importance that this slow advance towards the heart of existence should in

deux fois cela est bon aussi

Je crois que des deux toiles de cyprès celle dont je fais le croquis sera la meilleure. les arbres y sont très grands et massifs. l'avant plan très bas des ronces et broussailles Derrière des collines violettes un ciel vert et rose avec un croissant de lune L'avant plan surtout est très empâté des touffes de ronces à reflets jaunes violets verts. Je t'en enverrai des dessins avec deux autres dessins que j'ai encore faits,

fact prove to be the search for an illumination which does not yet exist, or the return towards a light glimpsed in earlier times and long since forgotten. The beginning and the end are inseparable in the search for true knowledge: "A return", wrote Martin Heidegger, "is a journey which leads back to a point of departure. The only man capable of returning is one who set out for his point of departure and, over a long period, bore upon his shoulders the full burden of the journey; the seeker could thus test the thing he sought, and himself arrive back less of a novice."

The point is not to enclose in some metaphysical system work which may indeed be a human appeal, but which is also the product of long and laborious effort. We must try to grasp the special nature of that adventure into which Van Gogh plunges body and soul, after his final attempt to find a place among men, to be accepted by men.

But we cannot avoid stumbling over the obsession with beginnings in the Dutch period which lasts from 1880 to 1886. During these years, Van Gogh's concern is to give expression to the earth, as well as to man and all his works.

Cypress-Trees
1889

The Brooklyn Museum
New York

"The white canvas has the fixed gaze of an idiot."

Driven out of what at least resembled a home, no matter how sordid its warmth, he first of all took refuge in Drenthe, the destination of the barges bringing their loads of peat along the canals. Then, at Christmas, he comes back to Nuenen, in Brabant, where his parents have settled. This is his return to the father, and to what existed before the Father. There is a sort of defiance in the glance he throws about him. He confronts his future task face to face, as though to rid himself of everything that encumbers or crushes him, or holds him back — and he does so as much as a protection against the incomprehension of his family as to conquer his ever-threatening melancholy. He enumerates his strengths and his powers — everything which will enable him to conquer his identity before that "other" who looks upon him as a dangerous shadow. In the spring of 1884, he writes: "Many painters fear the white canvas, but a white canvas fears a true and passionate painter who dares — and who has successfully defeated the fascination of the idea 'you are incapable of anything'"; and he adds: "life itself also always presents us with an infinitely banal white surface which discourages and leads us to despair: an absolutely virgin surface, as virgin as the white canvas on the easel. But no matter how banal, how vain, or how dead life may appear, the man possessed of faith, energy, and warmth, will not, knowing what he does, allow himself to be paid with false courage."

The two years in Nuenen are years of confrontation between white and black. The "infinitely banal" white is nothingness. The black is death. It is between those two empires of negation that life is somewhere hidden. Here, shadow adopts a particular form. It is no longer the contradictory mirror, reflecting white and black one after the other. On the contrary, it becomes an original ground which excludes both white and black. The whole of Van Gogh's effort at this period is a grandiose attempt to restore to shadow its rightful kingdom. For man can tolerate neither complete light nor the brilliance of the sun. As Antonin Artaud will put it, dread is born of "the torrid truth of a noon-day sun". But neither can man tolerate the depth of the shades, or the opacity of a starless night. Our domain is that of transparency, in other words of dusk, the joint refusal of midnight and noon. In the copy of *The Sower*, he reveals it indirectly by showing dusk to be the only defence of man's condition against the gulf of the

Thicket in the hills
1889

van Gogh Foundation
Amsterdam

night: dusk escapes time since it has neither beginning nor end, and because it never reveals at what moment the agony of day is over and the birth of night begins. While at Nuenen, Van Gogh seeks to portray the time of dusk, since it is our time. Later on, in Provence, as he glides towards the shores of eternity, he will bestow another tone upon that major theme taken from J.-F. Millet. This is how Michel Guiomar describes the picture of 1888: "Behind the sower, in an apocalyptic back-light, we see the sunset, in an atmosphere of dusk; a circle of light surrounds him; what does he sow − death; at any rate, death haunts both the man and his work. A similar back-light surrounds the tree, a dead tree, his neighbour and his double, the only other figure in the landscape, which both shelters him and threatens him with a dead branch. The man becomes a dead tree; the tree a spectre. Both are sowing nothing other than a link in the chain of life, a renewal of Birth and Death; and it is thus that the transcendence of a simple twilight spreads over the Funereal, the Unwonted, the Apocalyptic."

In Nuenen, the Apocalypse has not taken up the place in Van Gogh's life that it will occupy in Provence; so far, it is no more than what Artaud calls "the slow genetic nightmare". The pictorial adventure is a struggle to give an image to what has no image, a form to what is formless − to that whole intermediate universe, the world of grey and of brown which is that of the earth, the world of flowing water and passing time, of space which is neither near nor far, but in that indeterminate zone to which only the initiate have access.

This crepuscular study begins with a long exploration within objects of that background to life which seems to escape both day and night, a profoundly mysterious background whose life remains enigmatic since it is for ever preserved from the perils of noon and the abyss of night. Van Gogh will attempt, through this enigma, to penetrate to the heart of the human condition. If peasants and weavers are the bearers of so striking a truth, it is because, through their intimate contact with objects and their familiarity with everyday life, they have come to resemble those innumerable "silent lives" which make up the day-to-day world.

That is the reason why all the work produced in Nuenen has such a vital unity. Winter landscapes, weavers at work, harvesters or wood-cutters, humble pottery, pathetic series of faces buried in the practicalities of ploughing, families grouped round the potatoes, hovels laid out in the flat of the land, a solitary sheaf abandoned in a field at dusk − all these are simply variations on the privileged theme of the relationship between the instant and eternity. Each and every one of these reproductions carries within it all the others. In this line of research, also, Millet remains an example for Van Gogh: he had been the first to flee the anecdote, the incident, the event, while at the same time appearing to hunt them down. And this might be the point at which to reflect upon the extraordinary fortune which the Norman painter's "Angelus" was to know. Beyond the picture itself and all the faded sentimentalism with

Starlit night
1889

Kunsthalle
Brême

which the fake rural pathos is charged, the humblest peasant could unconsciously detect the relationship between himself and that ancient humanity of which he was a direct descendant. Like Millet, Van Gogh sought to give expression to the ancestral roots which attach men to the land they work, as though, beyond history, beyond the disasters and the deaths of which we are victim, there remained an irreducible truth, the impalpable trace of a creative act of which each life is a fragment. What Van Gogh is here describing is the rigorous complicity of a creation which keeps alive the dialogue between man, beasts, things, the sky, and the sea. It is the creation which existed before fragmentation and the frontiers of reason. There is no essential difference between the face of a man, a resting cow, a tree standing erect against the wind, the architecture of the weaver's loom, or the solitude of household utensils. Taken together, these created, living elements are part of the same movement, the same hidden palpitation.

The enormous effort to enter into this movement is accomplished in a state of violence, of patience full of burning fever: Van Gogh sees it as the only means of erecting an effective barrier against the erosion of which he is victim, and whose unremitting tension never leaves him in his family circle. But it is the only way, beyond the ordinary field of human cares, to recreate himself and finally to reach a permanent shelter. The shelter in which no words, no vain passions, no doubts may reach him. The great difficulty is how to live such a discovery, the only rampart against those absurdities "which transform society into a kind of madhouse, a world turned upside down". There is also the difficulty of contemplating both intimate reality – that with which Van Gogh has become familiar through knocking like a beggar at the dark door of destiny and of things – and the confusion of the world of other people, that broken horizon in which artifice, lies, negation reign supreme. He must bring about a true reconciliation between that other life, so suddenly revealed, and life incarnate, where others have their place. So that he may answer this question and at last comprehend what is engraved in the heart of this earth, Van Gogh leaves Nuenen, having exhausted all that was open to his gaze and to his imagination; for incarnation is men, and women, and children who work, suffer, embrace, separate; incarnation is those vast human communities where passions burn in great and visible fires. He must discover whether the humble truth discovered amongst the ploughmen and the weavers is merely a dream, or whether it retains . its substance and its ferment in the turbulent city.

The departure from Nuenen thus represents both a trial and a search for confirmation. The difficult union, the tragic harmony between man and the earth which Van Gogh believes he has made out amongst the work and the landscapes of Brabant may not survive in the midst of urban turmoil. What if it was nothing more than the product of a solitude which consoles itself with familiar day-dreams? Antwerp and then Paris will be the mirrors in which Van Gogh will seek the image of his true homeland, "the place where you feel really at home".

Sheaves of Corn
1885

van Gogh Foundation
Amsterdam

"There remain depths where melancholy persists."

At the end of 1885, shortly after arriving in Antwerp, Van Gogh is delighted with the man he has become after three years of solitary work: "As a young man, I had the appearance of an overworked intellectual; now I look like a bargee handling old iron. It's no easy thing to change your physical constitution in order to produce a thick skin." Thus the man who had been flayed alive in the Borinage, Etten and The Hague could now contemplate, without the slightest tremor, his face in the mirror. The peasants and the landscapes which he had relentlessly tracked down in the solitude of Nuenen had now bestowed upon him their hard immobility, their untiring strength, their earthy weight. In a sense, it is true to say that he had fed himself on the earth, on the human gaze, on faces worn by the patience of centuries; but on the earth before all else. A few weeks after getting to Antwerp, he confesses: "Since I arrived here, I have had only three hot meals; the rest of the time, I have eaten nothing but bread. A diet like that makes you a keener vegetarian than is good for you. Especially since I had to get by in the same way in Nuenen, for six whole months."

The hardness he has acquired shows as a major withdrawal. It is now the season when the wind rises, and when one must leave in order to discover elsewhere the state of one's self and of the world. In the winter of 1885-1886, he leaves the frozen countryside, where in any case a suspicious priest was causing him a certain amount of bother, and takes a room in Antwerp, in the hope of being able to sell a few canvases. The sight of the town enchants him: the ships, the museums and the women restore some pattern to a world where it may be possible to discover a little warmth. It was a winter of waiting and of impatience, of impairment of both his body and his nervous system: "I absolutely must recover my strength... I am suffering from a general weakening... I have made myself worse by smoking a lot − and I did it to deceive my stomach..."

The move to Antwerp was a step towards Theo, his last protection and his true guardian. For a long time, he has been asking his brother if he can go to stay with him in Paris. Theo is a possible intermediary in the painful dialogue between the painter and his family, he is the comforting replica of a father who, as the years go by, has retreated further into silence and disavowal. In May 1886, Van Gogh is in Paris. His stay there lasts for just under two years, long enough to transform his long Dutch search through the theatres of shadow into an exploration of the delirium of colour. But Paris is above all a liberation and an end to his solitude: with Theo he will discover Montmartre and its mound, as well as the

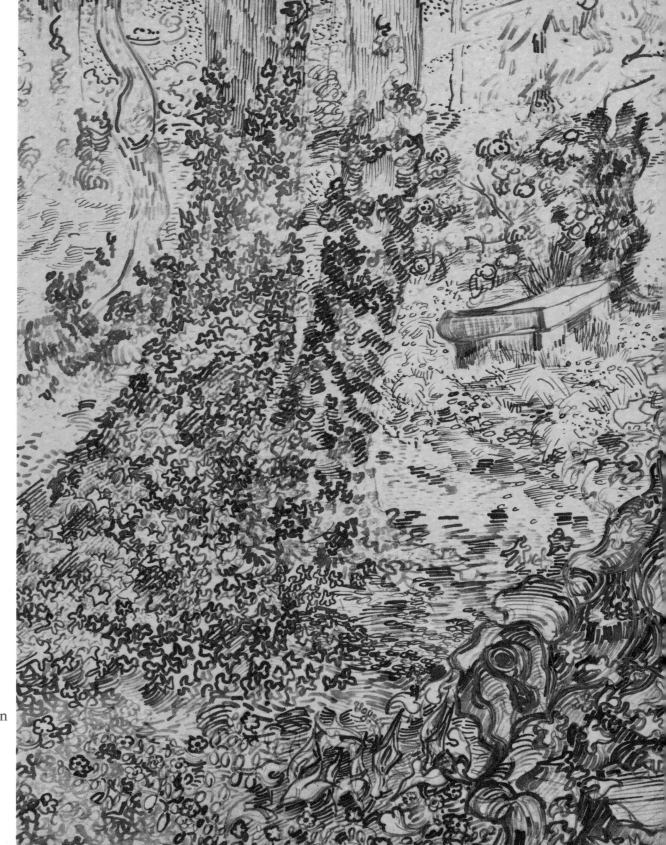

The stone seat
1889

van Gogh Foundation
Amsterdam

strange ant's-nest of a century drawing to its close. He is completely unfamiliar with the customs and contradictions of this society in which money will buy anything, where everything rots, where everything ferments; he is uncivilised man at the cross-roads of this hurried universe in which old memories hardly have a place. He cleanses himself of Holland, of its rains, and its charms; he also cleanses himself of himself. Above all, he comes to realise the hazards and the risks of the painter's art. There are many round him who, like him, will lose their reason and their being because of it. Once again, work is the only thing which can force him from the obsession of the consuming city.

    Vincent Van Gogh did not go to Paris in order to shut himself away in the mortal cluster of his dreams, as he had done in Nuenen. Now he has need of his fellow-artists, and he feverishly attaches himself to the immense artistic flowering, represented by Degas, Renoir, Monet, Sisley, Pissarro, and many others. But his real companions are Seurat and Signac: like him, they are haunted by the idea of metaphysical painting, by a representation of reality which plunges the creator into the inexpressible depths of the self. It is through them that he experiences the truth of colour, and that – having conquered shadow, having penetrated black and white, having exhausted the paths which lead from one to the other – he will perceive all the intoxication of blue, and yellow, and green, and red.

    Holland had provided him with the necessary substance of his life, she had brought him back to original matter. Paris provides a language which enables him to organise that substance, to give form to matter. He tries his hand at all the experiments he learns from his Impressionist friends. He borrows, somewhat haphazardly, without knowing what the borrowings will make of him, nor he of them. At any rate he frees himself from any doubts he might still have had about his technique or about his ability to transcribe the whole of what he hears around him. His working days are filled with exercises in which he shows that he can paint in the style of Manet, Renoir, Cézanne, Pissarro, or Signac. In the summer of 1887, he gets to the point of asking himself what remains of Van Gogh in the midst of this curious exchange. The question finds its answer in the admirable series of self-portraits in which the man contemplates himself, neither in haste nor in friendship, but with a fierce and pitiless sincerity. In these canvases and drawings, who contemplates whom? Is it Van Gogh looking upon his desert, his riches, his regrets, his future? Or is it the man in the picture, the man who has replaced the white of the canvas, who examines the artist with pity, with fury, with remorse? It is a fascinating gallery into which this being introduces the double he himself has created, but in which he does not recognise himself – or sees himself only too clearly.

    This portrayal of the self carries within it the sign of separation and of departure. Van Gogh quite obviously sees in his portrait a man who is poisoned and cursed. Paris is a drug. It brings together all the enchantments needed to dissolve the humble, fragile truth conquered with such difficulty during his years in Holland. Paris is history, an incoherent juxtaposition of all the roads imagined by men as a means of escaping from their own terror, of turning their attention away from themselves.

Self-Portraits
1887

van Gogh Foundation
Amsterdam

le jardin de Daubigny

Eternity has no place in these days and these nights given over to work, to pleasure, and to dreams. It is the land of men divided, torn away from the intimacy of their own warmth. It is a place where good and evil are the good and evil of all. And the reassurance which comes from apparent friendship, the turbulence of the streets, and the flow of words is bought at too great a price for a man to feel at ease. Van Gogh says so repeatedly to Theo once he is set up in Provence; Paris is the capital of wretchedness, and the greatest wretchedness is to have to live through a misfortune that one has not created for oneself. But Van Gogh, a child of Groot-Zundert and of Nuenen, will recognise no other tragedy than that for which he has himself fixed the limits. He is prepared for his body to be destroyed, for his brain to be torn apart, for his whole being to be smashed − but he insists on remaining the creator of his own catastrophe.

As soon as he arrives in the Midi, towards the end of the winter of 1888, he writes to Theo: "I was undoubtedly heading straight along the road to paralysis when I left Paris. That struck me clearly afterwards. When I had stopped drinking, stopped smoking so much, when I gave up reflecting instead of trying not to think, my God! What depression and what despondency." Provence will bring him back to himself, to his disaster and to his inalienable joy.

Cypress-Trees
1889

Kröller-Müller Stichting
Otterlo

The thatched cottage
1890

van Gogh Foundation
Amsterdam

Four men walking along the road
1890

van Gogh Foundation
Amsterdam

"No matter how black the devil, there is always a way of looking him straight in the eye."

The light in Holland had within it a fleeting whiteness, which gave the impression of an inhabited infinity, but which was in fact always closely related to shadow, like the negative form of black, or like some metal which no spiritual alchemy could restore to its original state, to its golden purity. The gold of the Low Countries is a nocturnal gold, which must be sought underground, or in the earth's dubious pits. It is the gold that glisters in the meditative lairs of Rembrandt's philosophers, and which lights up the distant face of Melancholy. There can be no doubt that Van Gogh had reflected at length upon this gold, for, as with all visionaries, his journey through this world of men had only one object: the conquest of the sun which bears within it promise for the future.

Others before him, rooted in the Northern mists, had sought out that same sun. At least three of them had lived an inner life inspired by a quest like that of Van Gogh, and all three had provided a different response — even though they had all the same inaccessible paradise. If one begins by examining the universe of Hieronymous Bosch, one is struck by the fact that, like Van Gogh, the painter of the "Millenial Kingdom" is the poet of genealogy. In the middle of the Garden of Eden, he places the original fountain of Life which gives birth to the sacred tree; this tree defines the three regions of knowledge: the infernal region in which secret knowledge flourishes, the vertical region which leads to celestial wisdom, and the horizontal region which is that of earthly knowledge. This triple fertility of knowledge is man's original state. The "Millenial Kingdom" is the description of a fall, of a collapse. Hell describes to us the fearful tribulations of those who distort divine creation, and tells of the slow fire which consumes a race forgetful of its original magic. Hell and Paradise mark out the limits of a continent whose name is Melancholy; men haunt its shores but never succeed in entering it, for it is a land of illusion. But Bosch shows us the paths and the bridges which make it possible for a few privileged men to regain the state of paradise, the state of the sons of the Sun; in other words, to link the beginning and the end of life, and thus to close the circle of immortality. Wilhelm Fraenger has pointed out that Novalis gives a modern expression to this theme in his "Song of the Dead": "Love alone has given us life, and we, with elemental fervour, impetuously mingle the floods of being, join heart to heart. The floods open voluptuously up, for the combat of the elements is the supreme life of love, the very heart of the heart. And mysteriously, in this flow, we express ourselves in the ocean of life, profoundly, in God. And, in his heart, the undertow draws us back to our own sphere, and the spirit of the supreme aspiration submerges itself in our vortex."

The Town Hall at Auvers
1890

van Gogh Foundation
Amsterdam

Houses at Auvers
1890

van Gogh Foundation
Amsterdam

For in Van Gogh, as in Novalis and Bosch, melancholy is the mediator which leads man from non-existence to existence, from division to identity. In order to follow this road, Bosch sets off in directions which may not be the ones chosen by Van Gogh, but which have strange similarities with them; he brings about the same symbolic distortion of reality by breaking the universe down into a series of coloured signs, of dramatic figures, each of which possesses its own secret. And it is beyond this distortion that begins the reign of rediscovered original joy, the joy of the first and the last sun.

Compared with the vast Odyssey of the imagination represented in the "Millenial Kingdom", Dürer's work takes on an infinitely more prosaic character. The themes and their expression are those provided by his age. And yet, one may find in Dürer a black sun which burns clearly in the Nuremburg painter's three most famous engravings: "Knight, Death and the Devil", "Saint Jerome in his cell", and "Melancholia". A patient examination of these three engravings reveals that the artist goes from the black sun − of which Melancholia is the symbol − to the golden sun which shines in the eyes of the knight, in the gaze of the hermit, in the face of the woman. "Melancholia" especially − a work to be compared with Van Gogh's numerous self-portraits − portrays the suffering of a consciousness unable to discover its distant aim, the drama of a rich imagination constantly brought up against the fleeting, derisory image of reality. But the sadness of the heart, the nostalgia of waiting, and the tragic aspiration towards the fullness of a world as yet unknown, all these are an appeal to inner power, which brings with it the promise of peace.

It is a peace that Saint Jerome achieves. Like Van Gogh, he is the repository of an ancient wisdom, and that wisdom is a form of nostalgia, for it no longer has any place in the adventures of men. But beyond this drama, a reconciliation nevertheless takes place. At the feet of the Saint, close to the book − and so to knowledge − a lion has come to rest. He has come to announce that henceforward a link may be made between living men and the memory of our beginnings. Nostalgia is thus both enriched and transcended, as in Van Gogh's self-portraits: in them, he is both the man who weeps because he has lost the source of his good, and the man who knows, whose life has a direction and will lead to a point which is neither nothingness nor the abyss.

Finally there is Rembrandt. He too is filled with the brown of nostalgia, invaded by the black of Melancholy; but he invents the golden sun by illuminating people and things from the inside. Van Gogh, like Rembrandt, is the painter of an eccentric light, which belongs to no physical structure, but which is wholly inspired by a metaphysical quest. For each of these Dutchmen, light is a quality of being. It is the product of an interior experience of which the physical representation is an immediate reflection, but which also refers to a vast archeology of life. And the painting of Rembrandt, like that of Van Gogh, bears witness to an increasing interiorisation of light. This light, the more clearly it achieves definition, serves also to define the world of shadow that each man bears within him. Rembrandt

Arum Lilies
1890

van Gogh Foundation
Amsterdam

A street at Auvers
1890

van Gogh Foundation
Amsterdam

Winter Landscape
1890

van Gogh Foundation
Amsterdam

Stone cottages at Chapolval
sketch of van Gogh on a letter

makes that shadow the projection of the living being on to the outside world, nature's response to the first action of original, solitary man. Van Gogh had meditated at length upon the paintings of his great predecessor, but he goes beyond Rembrandt by bestowing upon light its true majesty, and by eliminating the areas of shadow – or, more precisely, transforming that shadow into light.

The Hospital park
1889

Norton Simon Foundation
Fullerton, California

Study of pine-trees
1889

van Gogh
Amsterdam

Pine-trees
1889

van Gogh Foundation
Amsterdam

Olive Grove
1889

Nationalgalerie
East Berlin

"I feel within me a fire which I must not let go out."

The common ground between Bosch, Dürer and Rembrandt is the land of nostalgia. The elect of the millenial Kingdom, the mysterious, subterranean old men of Amsterdam, their flesh heavy with Melancholy, inhabit the universe of regret. Bowed under the weight of history, steering through the imaginary of a golden age, gone never to return, they confront the slow disintegration of time with the ephemeral face of heroic reverie. Before the disasters and the disorders of the seasons, they announce a gaze withdrawn from the clamour of the world. Once the bitterness of nostalgia is exhausted, there remains only a strange presence beyond regret. The road to knowledge does not lead to chaos, or to nothingness, or to madness. It gives out in a magical, painful consent.

In Bosch, it is the feeling of irremediable separation between the human condition, and the land of knowledge and power. Wilhelm Fraenger has written: "Bosch shows us man in all his nakedness, floundering in the inadequecies, the weaknesses, and the betrayals of his animal nature – a being who nevertheless was destined to penetrate the sublimest realms of the mind."But beyond the nakedness begins the smile. For Dürer, it is the certainty of the fragmentation of creation, of the impossible reconciliation of nature and the human heart, as expressed in the master of Nuremburg's last water-colour, a painting of the end of the world. But behind the fragmentation, the uncreated architecture of the gods appears. With Rembrandt, the most ordinary nude (though particularly the heavy, and yet fugitive, Bathsheba) shows the impossibility of going beyond nostalgia, the inability of our unfortunate nervous system to transcend the awareness of what is forever lost. Above all, it deprives knowledge of its glory.

The root of this nostalgia lies in the certainty that the human mind is the depository of a memory within whose labyrinth all knowledge of the future of life is hidden. During the three intensely creative years in Nuenen, Van Gogh, like Bosch, Dürer, and Rembrandt, excavated all the folds of that memory; the two years in Provence will be a long and painful journey towards that gulf which is beyond memory, towards the original explosion which is the source of life. It is as though, in violence and penury, Van Gogh tore out from the depths of his being that nostalgia, the constant presence – in daily life, in sleep, and in wakefulness – of a horizon with which communication is no longer possible. If this work touches us so cruelly today, if it goes so forcefully against the grain of our familiar dreams, our fantasies, and the indigence of our day-to-day desires, it is because it exists beyond the universe of regret, which is our special spiritual home; it is because it invites us to make the impossible break with the thousand threads woven into us from birth by the flesh and its weariness, history and its personal refuges,

Study of pine-tree
1889

van Gogh Foundation
Amsterdam

A path through the pines
1889

van Gogh Foundation
Amsterdam

desire and its contradictory wanderings. In opposition to the land of nostalgia, which our civilisation, through doubt and heartbreak, has created over the centuries, Van Gogh sets up a magic land, open upon creation to come, and not upon the destruction of the past. It may be that his departure for Provence came only when he knew that he was finished with the "Ancient World", when he believed himself capable of setting up a new alliance with so far unformulated forces which, from Spring to Autumn and from Winter to Summer, might bring into being a world as yet unknown.

The Dutch period has seen the exhaustion of the field of knowledge. The severe reality of his life, symbolising his approach to the world, was one that Van Gogh had embraced in a total act of love, so that it should reverberate throughout the whole of his being. Provence brings the exploration of a new knowledge, going beyond men, and giving expression to the star-filled night and the intolerable silence of stones. In fleeing Paris, Van Gogh gets away from the constant distraction to which the great city condemns him, as well as from the daily contact with a world of masks and disguise. That, at any rate, is how it appears to him: the city is a cancer, slowly eating away his painfully acquired powers, an alien voice whose questions are absurd, the answers equivocal, the temptations ambiguous.

In Arles, he is completely restored to himself. His road is laid out before him, and it is interesting to note that in his letters from Provence, the great internal torment, whose echoes could be heard throughout his years in Holland, seem to be calmer. Not that the tragedy in which he is plunged has been rid of its original fever. But rather that he is now caught up in a succession of revelations in which he no longer has to make choices or clarify obscurities. He has only to expose himself to that light, whose flame will consume him, but which will in the end become the captive of his unnamable passion. For such is the meaning of his final struggle: the flame which remains beyond our reach, the sun which denies man and all his works, the energy which seems to act outside the derisory field of our fortunes and our influence − all of these, which make up the other world, must be forced to lose themselves, and to dissolve into the breath and the hope of men.

Such a constraint is wholly defined by the creative act. From now until his death, Van Gogh's life is an insane fury for work. From now on, the themes of his art are of small importance: some are old themes which once more evoke his former links with the land, with those who work the earth, with things; other themes are seemingly new, to do with figures and flowers, scenes of working life, or life on the road. From the start, his entry into the kingdom of the sun leads to the vigorous destruction of subject-matter in his painting. His subject is now painting itself, the secret concealed in line, colour, the architecture of space.

All the rest, the weariness of everyday life, is no more than the price which must be paid to achieve such penury. Van Gogh's confidences on the frightful conditions in which he lives are no longer a protest, but merely a matter of fact, an indication of the pitiful glance cast upon those signs of happiness which must now for ever belong to another world. His appeals to Theo, his money difficulties, the unsatisfactory circumstances of his life in Arles take second place to his desire not to have to worry about his ability to buy paint, and not to have to waste time on the stupid irritations of material organisation. Each morning, despite hunger, sleeplessness, and physical pain, he remains fascinated by the spectacle before his eyes; his great fear is to miss that fleeting moment when objects begin to speak and reveal their elusive mystery.

Tree in blossom
1888

van Gogh Foundation
Amsterdam

"If I were to be pushed remorselessly towards suicide, I should end up by accepting it."

So that he may give himself entirely to his work and no longer be a prey to those terrible forces which confront him, Van Gogh seeks to hand over responsibility for that part of himself that still binds him to other men. It would be a way of breaking with the frightful solitude from which he has always suffered, but which, with the years, has become an ever-increasing obstacle to his dialogue with the light. Whence his dream of a community of artists, of a spiritual village in which a group of men, like him delivered from ambitions and temptations, would protect each other against the dread of the half-perceived abyss, and against the disorders of the imagination. But when Gaugin sets himself up in Arles, it is a matter of one solitude planting itself side by side with another solitude. This produces a misunderstanding which is all the more serious for having come at a time when Gaugin has not yet experienced the power and the tragedy of art. He has not yet reached the threshold which Van Gogh came to long before, and which leads into the heart of forbidden territories.

At this point, Van Gogh heads for more simple ways. Perhaps he remembers those old medieval pictures of the garden of madness, or tries once more to become one of those innocents who used to be put on board the ship of the mad so that, in each town in turn, men should take charge of their affliction and their joy, and protect them; at any rate, he makes the simple, harmless gesture that immediately brings him back to a state of innocence: he mutilates his ear.

The gesture is banal, but for him marks the beginning of a hitherto unknown peace and reveals with a staggering intensity the portrait of "the man with his ear cut off". That mutilation is after all no more than the logical development of his unending search for the self, which is not so much a desire to destroy as to achieve self-denial. The juxtaposition of the self-portraits reveals the obsession with the naked face, the need to reduce man to a sign. And yet, in any face, every feature has its significance; he must therefore reduce the appearance of the face to its essential structure, but without in any way destroying the powerful presence of each of the elements which make it up. Men of the Renaissance had been obsessed by the same problem; the work of Leonardo da Vinci, like the writings of Paracelsus, show them trying to resolve it by the destruction of surface appearances, by the attempt to reveal what lay beneath the mask, and what, in the darkness of the inner tissues, expresses the slow demands of life.

Study of fir-trees
1889

van Gogh Foundation
Amsterdam

Van Gogh treated himself as those men of the Renaissance had treated the depths of the human body. He tried to use himself as an *écorché*, revealing, beneath the calm order of the skin, of the human shell, the bloody palpitation of the inner life. In his obsession with his own face, what he sees is what he can sacrifice without destroying the irreducible. His ear is symbolic of this fact. The gesture was not at all the result of a moment of observation or of abstraction. It was rather the product of extreme concentration, coming at the end of that uninterrupted series of sacrifices through which he had reduced his physical presence, his worldly existence, to the limit. But, at the same time, the ear was an act of defiance and a cry for help.

The act of defiance is the gift he makes of his flesh to a wretched military prostitute, and, through her, to all those men and women for whom he has never ceased to bear a violent, indestructible love. A souvenir, he will call it, but it is much more than a souvenir, it is a gesture of gratitude, as though, by giving his ear to the immense mass of the poor, to all those exiles of heart and of mind who have always been his companions, he was appealing to them to recognise him once and for all as one of them, to accept him as the great messenger of innocence. But beyond his defiance, there is a manifest need to be done with the degrading bondage of his days and his nights. Since a community of artists is an impossible hope, he will do well to take refuge in the community of the asylum, amongst the most afflicted and the most abandoned of men.

In the asylum, beneath the stupid or compassionate eye of those looking after him, Van Gogh discovers a world of tenderness. And yet the life is frightful: the semi-imprisonment, the promiscuity of the sick and the mad, the vulgarity of the environment, the abandonment, the disgrace of the food, such are the factors which mark out the frontiers of this hell. But it is a hell which he sees only through a sort of mist. Now, as always, his one concern is to keep going. This man who has always been tempted to give up, who has often felt himself drifting down the slope to suicide, has greater strength than ever for the continuation of his work. What is important is not to stop: "It is curious that, whenever I try to reason with myself and to understand my situation − why I came here, and how in fact it was just an accident like any other − a terrible dread and horror take hold of me and stop me from thinking."

Van Gogh was always very clearly aware of what is called his madness. He knew it only in its most banal and immediate form: madness is separation, it is a break with the self and from that break with the self is born in its turn a break with the world of other men. Such is not his case. In his letters from Arles, he often speaks of "true life", which would surrender men to their own passion, which would lead them back to wisdom and to earthly fervour. But this true life is absent: the existence of others is a disguise, and it is no tragedy to be separated from them. There is no trace here of what Ronald Laing calls ontological insecurity, the withdrawal of the self. On the contrary, all the evidence shows that as the months go by, first of all in Arles, and then in Saint-Rémy, the extreme concentration of his mind leads him towards a more fundamental certainty of his own being.

Garden and houses at Auvers
1890

van Gogh Foundation
Amsterdam

"At night, I go outside to paint the stars."

Karl Jaspers has described at length the life led by Van Gogh from his arrival in Provence until his death in Auvers-sur-Oise. He has traced the slow disintegration of a man systematically exposed to all the chill winds of the mind, and in whom mortal toils progressively erode what modern analysts call identity. This erosion means that Van Gogh's road is one of contraction, leading to a profound unity of which death is the natural conclusion. After the tragedy of the cut-off ear, there is a kind of practical abandonment to the circumstances of life: Van Gogh refuses to take any interest in all the problems which filled his days, the difficulties of finding somewhere to live, of feeding himself, and hands over responsibility for his daily life to anyone who is prepared to accept it. What does it matter to him where he sleeps, what he eats, what his clothes are made of? This is the beginning of a fundamental trial. He is now face to face with the sun which is beyond life, with the fire whose power can be diminished by the most intensive work. His only obsession is with whether his body can stand up to the demands of his desire. "My feelings in a state of exaltation have a taste for preoccupations with eternity and eternal life"; the betrayals of a tired body, the incoherence of language shared with others are an alien burden which prevent him from glimpsing the face of eternity. The phrase "on the threshold of eternity" expresses the drama of all that encumbers life and makes it impossible to discover the true image of another peace, of another light. The disasters of solitude (but of a perverted solitude, ceaselessly invaded by others) are joined by disasters of memory; the mature man discovers what existence has made of him, and what pitfalls the past has insidiously dug for him. For every man is a geology, though an impure geology: the white passion of childhood becomes coated with black and with grey; tossed about through chance encounters and curiosities, great desires are eaten away by strange acids, torn apart by strange torturers; the images which furnish the new-born mind fail to find the sovereign incarnations which would give them sense and substance. And at the start of adulthood, when man emerges into the blinding sun of that interminable middle period between a long adolescence and old age, he realises how far he is from being complete.

And what Karl Jaspers calls Van Gogh's schizophrenia is the keen awareness of all that incompleteness that he, like any being sensitive to death, bears within him. The death of others, the death of familiar landscapes. In Arles, he dreams at length of his birth-place and of the garden in

Wooded landscape
1889

van Gogh Foundation
Amsterdam

Corner of the park at the Hospital
1889

van Gogh Foundation
Amsterdam

Steps in the park
1889

van Gogh Foundation
Amsterdam

Groot-Zundert. He dreams of them for they are now for ever abolished lands, the landscapes of exile. Baudelaire had already celebrated the land of non-return, that memory which can only be a burning sword in the gaping flesh. But that "nevermore", that certainty that all which humbly and feebly binds a being to his origins must crumble, had never been used by Van Gogh to nourish his melancholy. He always knew that his melancholy was never far off, and held itself ready to invade him and lead him to despair. His faith was always stronger than melancholy: "All I seek in painting is some means of extricating myself from life."

The thing he fears is not the danger of going under. It is rather that he should not be attentive enough to the mysterious signs made to him through painting by that unknown, that strange sky, which is both empty and densely populated, and from which nothing will ever distract him. Thus the incidents which, day after day and night after night, make up his biography, lose their importance. What matters is the bitter struggle to make images spring into the light of day, to deliver oneself – as a woman delivers herself of her baby – in an act more like an inexpressible joy than a deep-felt suffering. The will here reaches a degree of concentration which makes the greatest demands upon the nervous system. The interior strength is such that no misfortune may prevail against it: "Instead of trying to represent exactly what I see before me, I use colour more arbitrarily to express myself with greater strength." For the so-called real world is no more than the reflection of a richness which the eyes of the visionary are alone capable of bringing into the light of day. "Express the thought of a forehead by the radiance of a clear tone upon a dark background. Express hope through some star. The ardour of a being by the radiance of the setting sun." Time brings other revelations, until suddenly this inaccessible and heart-rending gaze turns to the tragedy of each living creature: "I have sought to express with red and green the terrible passions of men." As Karl Jaspers has pointed out, the miracle of Van Gogh is his attitude in face of illness: "he dominates it in a masterly manner."

But in this confrontation with the absolute, there is no prophetic aspiration. Neither is there any break – as might be expected from his illness – between the confused illumination of childhood and adolescence, and the fiery labours of Nuenen or the revelations of Provence. The further he journeys towards his end, the more faithful he is to his original inspiration, which is that of innocence and humility. The intolerable thing about Paris had been the vanity of its artists, leading them to place their calling so high as to be out of the reach of ordinary men. But whether in the fields of Arles or the orchards of Saint-Rémy, Van Gogh remains what he had been in the water-logged earth of Holland: a poor artisan condemned despite himself to assume responsibility for a truth for which, in all honesty, he thought he could be no more than the depository.

The countryside at Auvers
1890

van Gogh Foundation
Amsterdam

"Healing comes from within."

Nothing is more fascinating than this struggle, night after night, to create outside of genius, to rediscover the most modest gesture of the most ancient of men. The reason why, right to the end, he remains obsessed by the canvases of Jean-François Millet is that the painter of Barbizon had succeeded in restoring the true accent to that elementary life. And this struggle, on which his true despair is founded, leads him to an ever-completer renunciation. In the end, everything gives way to the juxtaposition of a few lines, a few colours: nature, like man, becomes enclosed in something which is almost non-existent, and yet which is the only essential presence.

But, as we see in the tragic hallucination of the crows and the field of wheat, this elementary universe is nothing less than a gigantic wound, an interminable scar condemned to reopen, and fester, and bleed. Van Gogh lived this tragedy to the full so that the calamity of creation might burst forth through his own disaster. There was no other way of knowing the immense, unending birth-pangs of this universe, than that of taking upon his own shoulders all that history enabled him to bear.

His recourse to the sun and the stars in the last months of his life is the symbol of his fusion with the inscrutable cycle of time, of his plunge into the eternal Return. There is no delirium here, no nightmare, no hallucination. Nothing but the certainty of a presence, and of the approach of that mystery to which, according to the Greeks, only Dionysos, "the mad god", holds the key.

Thatched Cottages
1890

van Gogh Foundation

Wooded bank of the Oise
1890

van Gogh Foundation
Amsterdam

udy of a peasant
90

n Gogh Foundation
msterdam

Vincent Van Gogh arrived in Arles on 21 February 1888. Gauguin joined him in October, and then left again in December, after that strange Christmas involving the mutilation of the ear. In March 1889, he was back in hospital, and in May he entered the asylum in Saint-Rémy; that is where he stays until May of the following year. What becomes of him during these two long years when every moment not stolen from him by physical concerns is devoted to strenuous effort, patience, and a passion to see? A man searching the sky, a mind given up to the torments of infinity. No doubt Van Gogh had, from the outset, obscurely realised that for the sublime to find its time and its place within him he would have to go from suffering to suffering, from sacrifice to sacrifice, until his body was finally subdued and could become a marvellously sensitive organism capable of reflecting the rays from a sun which our jaded eyes may no longer perceive. And it is surely true that he had less fear of mental breakdown than of a weakening of the flesh which would gradually make it insensitive to that radiant light. For madness, after all, is a word invented by others, the horizon with which others surround him. But this body which, from earliest childhood, he had never ceased to track down (did not the extreme solitude of his early years reflect the basic need to protect his being against the eyes and the gestures of others), this body in which his fundamental obsessions had slowly become engraved, was his sole asset, his only power. But since it was a body of love, it was also a body of death. And the need to continue would cease to exist when he became unable to go further upon the road towards the dazzling light, when he was no longer the vigorous mirror of ecstasy.

"Forward, forward" – Van Gogh had frequently written it to Theo. In the peace of Auvers-sur-Oise in July 1890, he had no further reason to go forward, for he could not do so without going astray. The burning spark, of which the murmuring cloud of crows must surely have been the last trace, had to be kept intact. During his summer in the Ile-de-France, he senses that the illumination is behind him, and that, bit by bit, an absence is invading a nervous system no longer able to keep his wealth of cruel knowledge within its human limits. It is the moment that Van Gogh chooses to enter that temporary death and to take his place in those special gardens which men reserve in their cities for all that fall. The death is contrived – not that of a man who falls, but, on the contrary, that of a being clearly contemplating his final chance of seizing the irremediable sweetness of things created. Perhaps the stars indicated that other world wherein was true life. The real abode was this dark and heavy earth, far from the voices and the silences of men; far from this world "so obviously thrown together in haste, on one of those poor days when the creator no longer knew what he was doing, when he did not have his mind on his work."

n the garden of the Hospital
889

an Gogh Foundation
msterdam

mais enfin là jusque là je vous suis et
mon père saisit bien cette nuance.
J'ai encore de là bas un cyprès avec une étoile

un dernier essai. — un ciel de nuit avec
une lune sans éclat Dans à peine le
croissant mince émergeant de l'ombre
projetée opaque de la terre — une étoile
à éclat exagéré si vous voulez, éclat doux
de rose et vert dans le cobalt outremer
où courent des nuages. En bas
une route bordée de hautes cannes
derrière lesquelles des alpines bleues basses
à crêches illuminées orangées
une vieille auberge et un très haut
cyprès tout droit tout sombre.
Sur la route une voiture jaune attelée
d'un cheval blanc et deux promeneurs
attardés. Très romantique
si vous voulez, mais aussi je crois

de la Provence. Probablement je graverai à l'eau forte celle là

Page of a letter from van Gogh

Contents

PRINTED IN FRANCE. IMPRIMERIE-RELIURE MAISON MAME, TOURS.